Mighty Machines

BULLDOZERS

Amanda Askew

QED Publishing

Words in **bold** can be found
in the Glossary on page 23.

Copyright © QED Publishing 2010

First published in the UK in 2010 by
QED Publishing
A Quarto Group company
226 City Road
London EC1V 2TT

www.qed-publishing.co.uk

A Catalogue record for this book is available from the British Library.

ISBN 978 1 84835 398 5

Written by Amanda Askew
Designed by Phil and Traci Morash (Fineline Studios)
Editor Angela Royston
Picture Researcher Maria Joannou

Associate Publisher Zeta Davies
Editorial Director Jane Walker

Printed in China

Picture credits
Key: t = top, b = bottom, c = centre, FC = front cover, BC = back cover

Alamy Images David R. Frazier Photolibrary, Inc 10l; **Getty Images** AFP/David Furst/Stringer 14l,
Jeff T. Green/Stringer 19t; **Istockphoto** Filonmar 6–7, Ivanastar 9t, Emre Ogan 12–13, Jowita Stachowiak
18–19, 22bl; **Komatsu America** 20–21, 21t; **Photolibrary** Age Fotostock/Dennis MacDonald 10–11,
22tl; **Shutterstock** BC, Buhanstov Alexey FC, Dmitry Kalinovsky 1, 8–9, Ownway 4–5, 22bc, Zolwiks 5r,
Jose Gil 13t, 22tr, Christina Richards 16b, Catalin Petolea 16–17, 22br; **US Air Force** Master Sgt Rickie
D. Bickle 14–15, 22tc

Contents

What is a bulldozer?

Bulldozers are mostly used on **building sites**. A bulldozer is a big **tractor** with a **blade** on the front. The blade is used to push things or cut into the ground.

A bulldozer makes the ground level before work starts.

A bulldozer has **tracks** instead of wheels. The tracks help the machine to move across rough ground. If a bulldozer had wheels, it would probably slip and slide.

A bulldozer has wide tracks. They stop the machine from sinking into the ground.

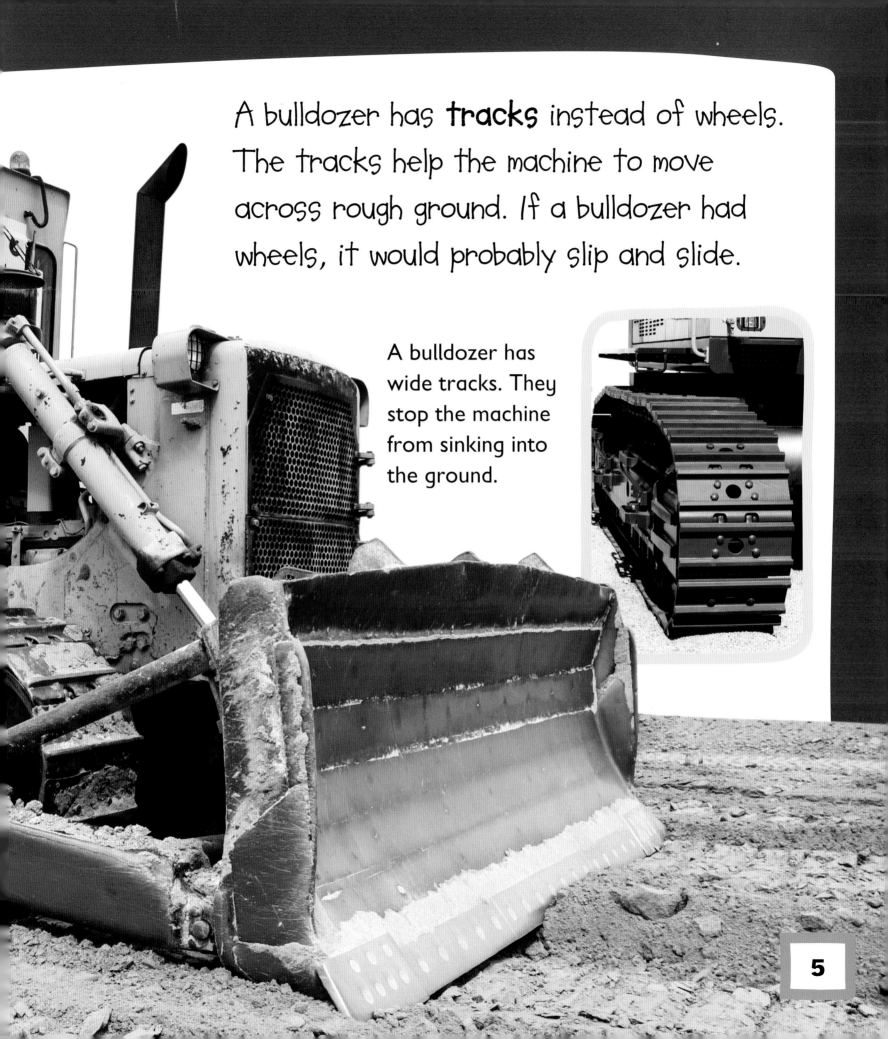

Parts of a **bulldozer**

A bulldozer has two main parts – a tractor and a blade. When the blade pushes downwards, it cuts into the earth. When the blade pushes forwards, it moves the pile of earth.

tractor

The tractor is the main part of the bulldozer. The driver sits in the cab and controls the machine.

blade

cab

ripper

tracks

7

Blades and rippers

The bulldozer uses its blade to spread out uneven earth. This makes the ground flat.

The blade is on the front of the tractor. There are many shapes and sizes of blade. Most bulldozers have a straight blade, but some have curved blades.

The **ripper** is a large claw on the back of the tractor. The ripper 'rips' into the ground and breaks it up.

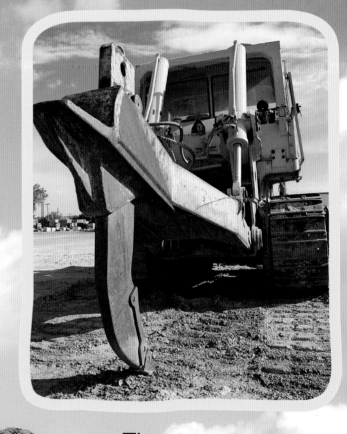

This ripper is about to break up the hard ground.

Building roads

Tarmac has to be laid on flat ground. A bulldozer flattens the ground so a new road can be built.

The bulldozer pushes and spreads huge mounds of earth to make the road flat.

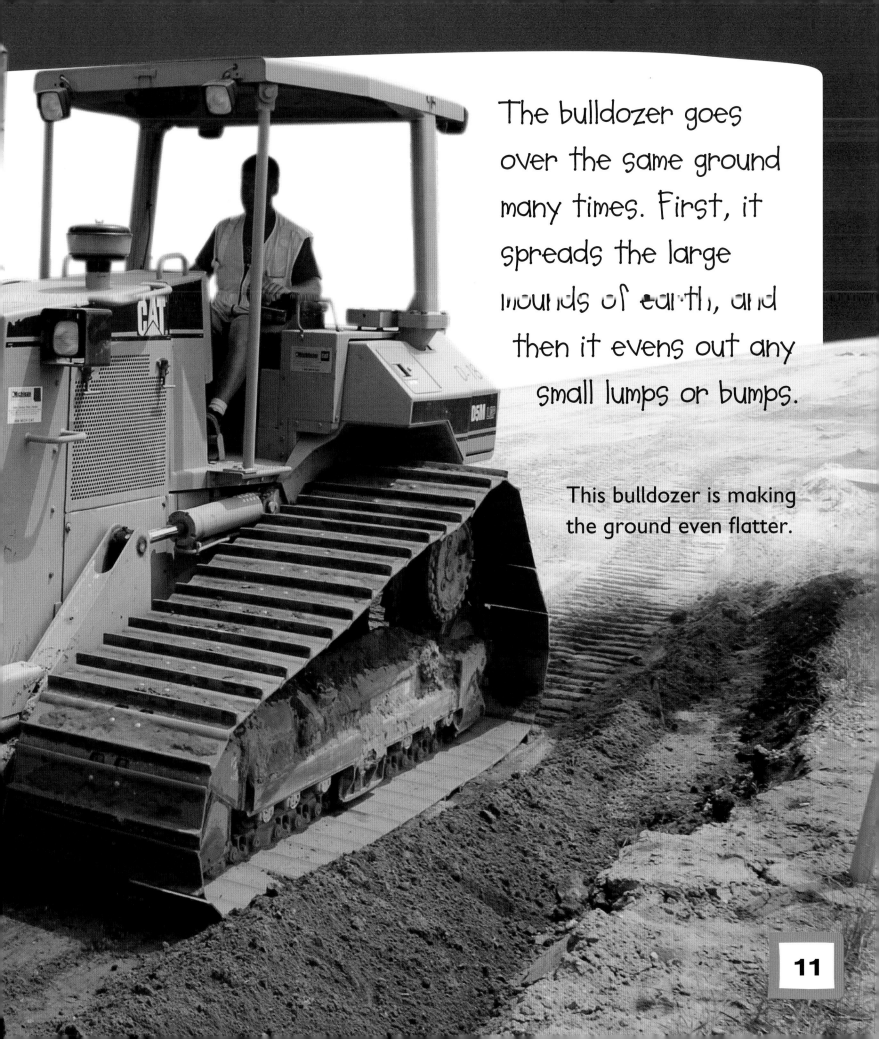

The bulldozer goes over the same ground many times. First, it spreads the large mounds of earth, and then it evens out any small lumps or bumps.

This bulldozer is making the ground even flatter.

Mining and quarrying

Large and small bulldozers are used at **mines** and **quarries**. They clear piles of rocks. The small machines can work where there isn't much room.

Some bulldozers use a special blade, called an 'SU blade'. The blade is so large, it can push piles of big rocks.

This SU blade turns up at the sides. The sides hold the rocks on the blade.

This machine is moving loose rocks.

In the army

Soldiers use bulldozers to clear a path through thick forests or across uneven land. Sometimes, a bulldozer blade is fitted to a tank.

These bulldozers and tanks are crossing rough ground.

The bulldozer is painted a dull colour, so that it looks like the ground and trees around it. This is called **camouflage**.

This bulldozer clears the ground so that the soldiers can build a new bridge.

On the **farm**

Some farmers use bulldozers to break up very hard ground. A **plough** cannot work when the ground is too hard.

The bulldozer is digging up the roots of a fallen tree.

16

A ripper is dragged through hard ground to break it up. The farmer can then plough the land and plant crops.

A ripper can have one spike or lots of spikes.

Ploughing the snow

Bulldozers make good **snowploughs**! The blade clears a path through the snow or ice. The tracks stop the bulldozer from sliding on the slippery ground.

A snowplough stops cars and people from being blocked in by the snow.

A train can clear a track much faster than a bulldozer!

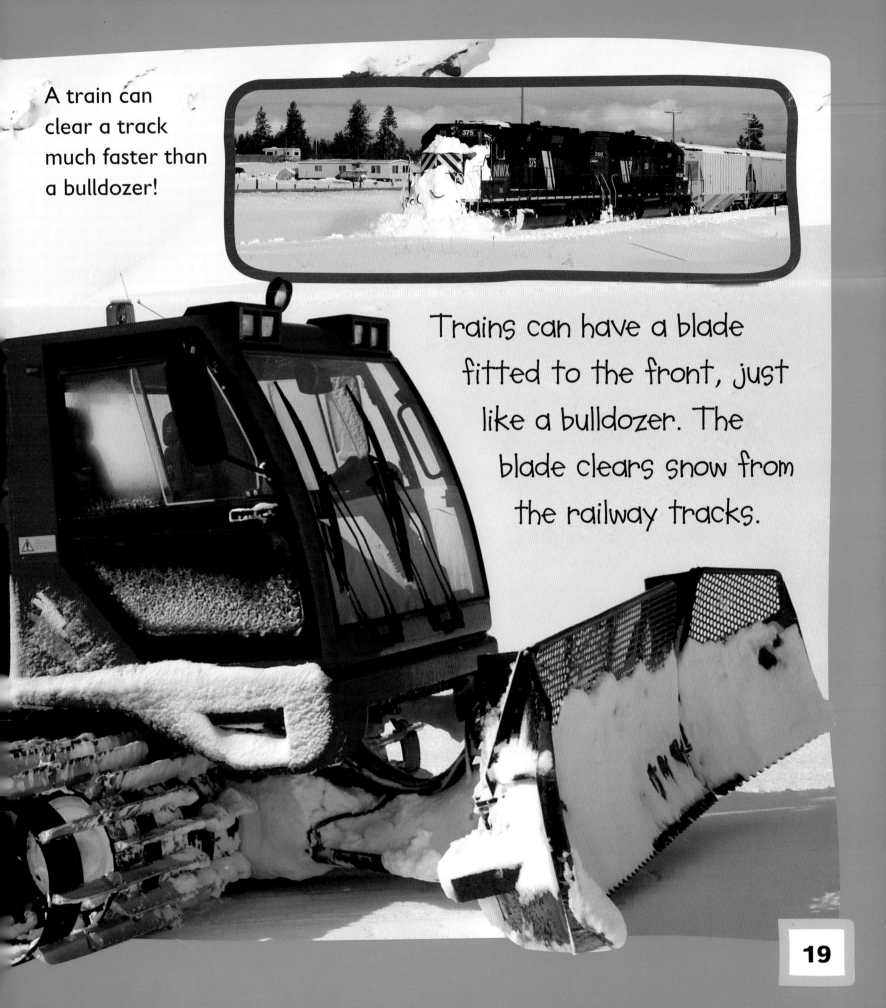

Trains can have a blade fitted to the front, just like a bulldozer. The blade clears snow from the railway tracks.

Biggest and smallest

The biggest bulldozer in the world is a Super Dozer. Its blade is 7 metres wide. Four adults could lie along it head to toe!

This monster machine can push 127 tonnes of rocks in one go. That's the same weight as 20 elephants!

The blade on this mini bulldozer is less than 70 centimetres wide – no wider than two and a half of these books laid end to end!

Small machines are perfect for working in small spaces.

Activities

- Here are three bulldozers from the book. Can you remember what they do?

- If you needed to break up hard ground, which attachment would you use? Why did you choose that attachment?

- Draw a bulldozer building a road. Which bulldozer did you choose? What colour is it? Who is driving it?

- Which picture shows a ripper?

Glossary

Blade
A large, flat attachment used for cutting or pushing earth.

Building site
A place where a house or other building is being built.

Camouflage
A way to hide something by making it the same colour as the place it is in.

Mine
A deep hole in the ground. Coal is often found in a mine.

Plough
A machine that turns over the soil to make it ready for seeds to be planted.

Quarry
A place where stone and sand are dug out of the ground.

Ripper
An attachment with a spike or spikes for breaking up hard ground.

Snowplough
A machine that is used to move snow from roads.

Tarmac
A hard material used to make the surface of roads.

Tracks
A long, metal band around the wheels on a bulldozer.

Tractor
A farm machine with big wheels.

Index